Biometric Technology

Mark Lockie

Heinemann
LIBRARY

www.heinemann.co.uk/library
Visit our website to find out more information about **Heinemann Library** books.

To order:
☎ Phone 44 (0) 1865 888066
🖹 Send a fax to 44 (0) 1865 314091
🖥 Visit the Heinemann Bookshop at www.heinemann.co.uk/library to browse our catalogue and order online.

First published in Great Britain by Heinemann Library, Halley Court, Jordan Hill, Oxford OX2 8EJ, a division of Reed Educational and Professional Publishing Ltd. Heinemann is a registered trademark of Reed Educational and Professional Publishing Ltd.

OXFORD MELBOURNE AUCKLAND JOHANNESBURG BLANTYRE
GABORONE IBADAN PORTSMOUTH NH (USA) CHICAGO

Designed by Tinstar Design (www.tinstar.co.uk)
Illustrations by Martin Griffin
Originated by Ambassador Litho Ltd.
Printed and bound in Hong Kong/China

ISBN 0 431 14885 6
06 05 04 03 02
10 9 8 7 6 5 4 3 2

British Library Cataloguing in Publication Data
Lockie, Mark
       Biometric technology. – (Science at the edge)
       1. Biometrics. – Juvenile literature
       I.Title
       570.1'5195

Acknowledgements
The Publisher would like to thank the following for permission to reproduce photographs:
Ancient Art and Architecture: p6; Art Directors & Trip: p43; Corbis: pp10, 37, 51; DK Images: pp16, 18, 20; Ed Stuart: p23; Eye Ticket Corporation: p33; Impact Photos: Eliza Armstrong p48, John Cole p5, Javed A. Jafferji p53, Andy Johnstone p28; Newham Council: p36; Photodisc: p54; Popperfoto: p50; Recognition Systems: p15; Robert Harding: p17; Sagem: p31; Science Photo Library: pp9, 11, 14, 19, 22, 24, 27, 30, 35, 44, 46, 55, 56; Shout Pictures: pp21, 38, 41; Trevor Clifford: pp8, 13, 39, 42, 52.

Cover photograph reproduced with permission of Science Photo Library/James King-Holmes.

Any words appearing in the text in bold, **like this**, are explained in the Glossary.

Contents

Biometric technology

Every human being on Earth is unique. Even identical twins, who may look exactly the same, have certain characteristics that vary, such as their **iris** patterns or the way in which they sign their names.

These characteristics are important because they can be used to help recognize people. One of the most common characteristics being used is the human **fingerprint**. It is highly unlikely that anybody else would have exactly the same fingerprint pattern as you. In fact, no two people in the world have ever been found to have exactly the same fingerprint pattern. This is why fingerprint evidence can be used in a court of law to show that a specific person was present at the scene of a crime.

Not all human characteristics can be used to identify a person. If you were to measure all the children in a school, for example, there is a good chance that many of them would be the same height. However, if you also weighed the children and noted the colour of their eyes, then the chances of any of those children having *exactly* the same characteristics are greatly reduced.

Powerful technology

Many companies, governments and scientists are taking this idea further. They are producing highly accurate biometric technology that can **automatically** recognize people from their unique characteristics. This technology does not normally look at characteristics like the height and weight of a person, but it may look in detail at a particular part of the body, such as the eye.

Once the biometric machine has recorded a person's characteristic, it compares it against records that are already in its memory. If it finds there is a strong match between the new characteristic and one stored on the file then it will recognize that person. If there is no match, then that person could be an **impostor** and is rejected.

You are most likely to have seen biometric systems in action in spy movies – perhaps where a person is not allowed access to computer files unless that computer recognizes their voice or iris pattern.

Slowly, the technology is making its way into everyday environments, like prisons, banks and hospitals. Even some schools are now using biometrics. For example, in the USA, Eagan High School in St Paul, Minnesota, is using fingerprint **sensors** to identify its students, so that they can take out books from the school library. The Royal Grammar School in Guildford, UK, is using fingerprint readers to protect certain areas, such as common rooms and music rooms, from thieves.

Biometric technology can be controversial. Some people are worried that if biometric systems become widespread, this powerful technology could be used to monitor people against their will. This book will explain how biometric technology works, and why it could greatly benefit society, if used in a sensible way.

The diversity of human beings is staggering. The science of biometrics relies on the fact that no two people are exactly alike, including twins.

What are biometrics?

The origins of the biometrics industry go back a lot further than its futuristic image might suggest. There is evidence that, many centuries ago, the ancient Egyptians used to identify people by measuring human characteristics.

Building the great pyramids of Egypt was a massive and complicated task which involved many thousands of workers. Each of these workers was entitled to certain **provisions**. However, some workers were not happy with their own quota, and attempted to get double rations by claiming to be somebody else. With so many people at work, there was no accurate way to tell whether or not a person was telling the truth.

Studies of the ancient Egyptians show that many of today's technologies, including biometrics, had their origins in this era.

To combat this problem, the Egyptians responsible for giving out the provisions began making records about each worker. As well as names, these records may have included details about the shape of a worker's face, his physical size, skin complexion and any other noticeable features, such as scars. Put together, this information could be used to check whether a worker was owed his provisions or was just a greedy **impostor**!

Egyptians versus the modern day

The main difference between the method being used by the ancient Egyptians and the method used by a modern biometric system is that today's biometric systems '**automatically**' recognize a person.

This difference is fundamental to the definition of a biometric. The official definition of a biometric is 'a measurable characteristic or behavioural trait of a live human being that can be used to automatically recognise or **verify** identity' (source: 'Biometric Technology Today').

While the Egyptians would have spent time searching through records and checking physical details to verify a person's identity, a modern biometric system uses special automatic **sensors** and computer technology to do this.

Nevertheless, the basic Egyptian principle of making records of human characteristics to confirm a person's identity is still applied in most modern biometric systems.

Unique human characteristics

There are many characteristics that are unique to each person's body. Some of these are ideal for measuring; others would be almost impossible to measure. An ideal biometric is quite easy to measure, is unique to one person and shouldn't change much over time. For example, once an **iris** pattern is created it stays constant throughout a person's life. Also, lots of interesting information can be extracted from its pattern using a sophisticated camera and a computer.

It isn't just body parts that can be measured using a biometric machine. The machine can also measure the way you do something, such as type at a keyboard or sign your name.

Although there are some more unusual biometrics which may be used in the future, including a person's unique smell, the shape of their ear or even the way that they walk, the main biometrics being measured today are:

- fingerprints
- hand shape
- face shape
- iris patterns
- palm prints
- **retina** patterns
- vein patterns
- voice
- the way a person signs his or her name
- the way a person types at a keyboard.

There are two main types of biometric – physical and behavioural. A **physical biometric** is a part of a person's body, such as a **fingerprint** or hand shape. A **behavioural biometric** is something that a person does, such as signing his or her name, or typing at a keyboard.

Humans are born with their physical characteristics, but behavioural biometrics are developed over time. Once developed, however, **behavioural characteristics** can be quite unique and surprisingly constant – this makes them ideal biometrics.

Why not DNA?

The set of instructions, known as **DNA**, that determine a human being's characteristics, are perhaps the most unique thing a person possesses. In fact, DNA is so unique that even tiny traces of it can be used as **forensic** evidence in a court of law, to prove whether a suspect was present at the scene of a crime.

However, despite the unique nature of DNA, it is not yet thought of as a biometric. This is because the process of obtaining a DNA sample (often by taking a **swab** from the inside of the mouth) and comparing it with a previous sample has not yet been fully **automated**. Of course, this may change in the future.

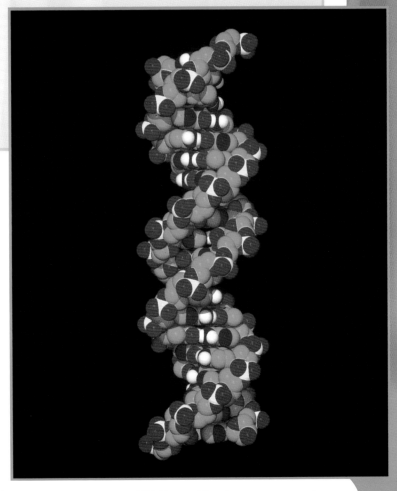

The extreme complexity of DNA would make it an extremely unique biometric. Unfortunately, it is not yet possible to automate the process of taking a sample and analysing the results. This means it is not yet classed as a biometric technology.

The biometrics industry

The biometrics industry didn't really get started until the middle of the twentieth century. At that time, researchers started publishing **papers** looking at whether various human features, such as the **retina** or the voice, could be used to recognize a person. As a number of these strands of research began to come together, the biometrics industry as we know it today was formed.

The biometrics industry is relatively young, and exciting scientific developments are still being made today. The early biometric systems took a while to catch on, and were far from perfect.

One of the very first biometric systems was developed in the 1960s by the Miller Brothers in New Jersey, USA. This system did not use complicated computer technology, but was a mechanical device, designed to **automatically** recognize people by measuring the length of their fingers!

Soon after this came a number of products that looked at other types of biometrics. In the 1970s, for example, the US Air Force awarded a number of contracts to Texas

Organizations, such as the FBI, were early users of biometric devices to increase security.

Instruments, a company that pioneered the use of systems that recognize people from their voices. Meanwhile, the US Federal Bureau of Investigation – the FBI – made use of **fingerprint** readers.

Iris recognition is one of the latest biometric systems to be launched commercially. A company based in the USA, called Iridian Technologies, started selling an iris recognition device in 1995, and claims it is one of the most accurate biometric systems available. This technology is now being used in many places: for example, in airports to allow special travellers to bypass long passport control queues by showing their irises to a reader.

As it became clear that recognizing people from their characteristics could increase security for companies and individuals, the biometrics industry grew rapidly. Today, many companies around the world are developing products for all sorts of uses.

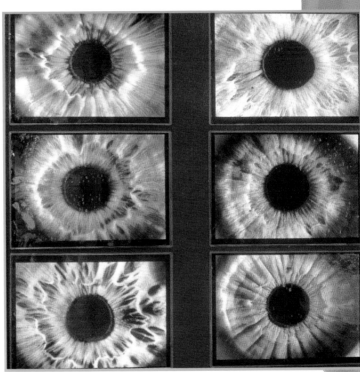

These iris images have been scanned as part of a computer recognition program. The images show the extreme variations in every person's iris pattern that can be detected by a biometric system.

'The truth is, early implementations of biometric technology were far from the perfect solution that many expected them to be. With hindsight, this was partly because expectations had been raised too high by over-enthusiastic industry claims.'

Julian Ashbourn, author of *Biometrics: Advanced Identity Verification – The Complete Guide*, 2000

11

If the world was full of biometric systems, life would be more secure, and it would also be much simpler. You certainly can't leave your biometric at home like you can a bunch of keys, and you cannot forget your biometric, like you can a password!

What's wrong with keys?

Keys have been around for many years, and are still by far the most popular choice for making everything from people's homes and cars to their offices or even their suitcases secure. More recently, items such as **swipe cards** and **PIN numbers** have been introduced as alternatives.

Sometimes, these items must be used together to increase security. For example, when you want to get money out of a bank, you often need both a card and a PIN number to prove you are the true account holder. This is more secure, because you don't just have to *own* something (in this case your card); you also have to *know* something (in this case your PIN number).

However, there is a problem with all these methods. Keys and cards can easily be stolen, while many people write down their PIN numbers and keep them with the bank card, or change them to obvious numbers, such as the year they were born. With passwords, many people use words that are simple to remember, such as the name of their town, partner or pet. This means that another person can easily guess them.

Something that you 'are', such as a fingerprint

Something that you know, such as a password

Something that you own, such as a key

Increasing level of security

Thieves have even been known to look over a person's shoulder as they are typing in their password or PIN, so they do not have to guess the number once they subsequently steal the person's card.

Although many of these thieves eventually end up paying for their crimes, the problem has grown serious enough for biometrics to become an important alternative. Because nobody has the same biometric characteristics as you, they cannot easily pretend to be you and attempt to take out money or access confidential information. Biometrics are the highest level of security possible, because they are something 'that you are'.

> 'It does seem reasonable that within the next five years, we will see a more wide-scale implementation of biometric systems within the banking sector.'
>
> Ron Coben, executive vice president, Bank United

Keys and passwords have an extremely important place in society, but they are easy to lose and forget. As biometrics are either part of your body or the way you do something, they are impossible to forget or lose.

Who uses biometrics?

We have seen that the main use of a biometric system is to gain access to something, whether it is a building, a theme park or information on a computer. In a way, a biometric can be thought of as a 'human key' to replace or work alongside normal keys, tickets or passwords.

Early biometric systems were generally very expensive. This meant that the only groups of people who could really afford to use them were those who needed to guard high security areas. These groups included the military, police forces and owners of nuclear power stations, for example.

However, as time has progressed, the price of biometric systems has dropped a great deal. This means that they are now available to many more people, from doctors in hospitals wanting to access a patient's **medical records** stored in a computer file, to people wanting to get money from a safe at their bank. For example, doctors in the Netherlands can now use fingerprint biometrics to access medical records on all patients suffering from burns injuries in the country. Not only that, but they can also access these records securely over the Internet.

Nuclear power stations need to be highly secure locations. This is why numerous facilities around the world rely on biometric technology to guard against possible intruders.

Of course, the biometric industry is still very young, so most of these ways of using biometric systems are not yet common. It is quite possible you've never knowingly seen a biometric system, but one day, it is likely that biometrics will be commonplace. Almost everybody will use their bodies as 'human keys', allowing them to get into their homes, offices and even their cars.

Police presence

Many of the world's police forces are strong supporters of the biometrics industry, and use the technology to prevent crime and catch criminals. Cameras have been used by the police to capture images of people's faces at sports stadiums, so that they can spot known criminals in a crowd. For example, a highly controversial face recognition scheme at the US Super Bowl in Tampa, Florida, recently identified nineteen people who were wanted by the police. Elsewhere, hand-measuring systems are used in many prisons to make sure that visitors leaving the jail are the same as the ones that came in, or to stop prisoners escaping!

The most successful biometric used by police forces, however, is the fingerprint. Fingerprints found at crime scenes are always checked to see if they already exist on police file. In the past this was a manual procedure, which took a long time. Today, thanks to sophisticated biometric technology, the process is **automated** and takes a matter of hours, rather than days or weeks.

Prisons are an obvious place to use biometrics. Here, a **hand geometry system** is used to check the identity of a person before allowing them through a turnstile.

Body parts

There are many parts of the body that can be measured by biometric systems. As we have seen, these include **fingerprints**, hands, faces, eyes and voices. Other common biometrics that are measured are not parts of the body, but are **behavioural characteristics**, such as the way a person signs their name.

When a biometric system looks at a particular part of the body, it often focuses on complex details, not immediately obvious to the human eye. For example, a fingerprint recognition system might look at the tiny markings in the skin called **minutiae**. A system looking at the **retina** will examine blood vessel patterns at the back of the eye.

Fingerprints

Fingerprints are the most commonly used biometric. They are formed before birth, as the hands develop. Fingerprints aren't actually formed in the skin, but are caused by ridges in the flesh underneath the skin. If you look at your fingerprint, you will see that it is made up of a complicated network of lines. It is quite easy to see how these lines create distinct patterns that are normally made up of **whorls**, **loops** and **arches**. It is much harder to see the large number of minor markings on the fingerprint – the minutiae.

Every fingerprint is different. On close inspection it can be seen that the patterns are made up from combinations of whorls, loops and arches.

Fingerprints are such a widely used biometric for several reasons. For example, not only are they easy for a biometric system to record (a person simply has to place their finger on a **sensor**), but they also change very little over time – unless of course the finger becomes badly scarred or damaged.

Although most people in the world have very easy to measure fingerprints, there are often noticeable differences between sexes, races and even the type of job a person does. Generally speaking, men have clearer fingerprints than women, Asian people have harder to read fingerprints than **Caucasians**, and manual workers have less clear patterns than office workers, due to the environment they work in. Therefore, the most difficult people for a biometric system to recognize are Asian women whose jobs involve manual work, while male, Caucasian office workers are the easiest.

Biometric systems must work with all races and genders, but they work best with Caucasian men that work in offices.

Hand

The human hand is the source of a number of different biometrics, and was the feature used for the earliest biometric systems. Generally, it is the unique shape of a person's hand or fingers that is used to identify them. However, as technology has advanced, even vein patterns on the back of a person's hand or their palm prints can now be measured.

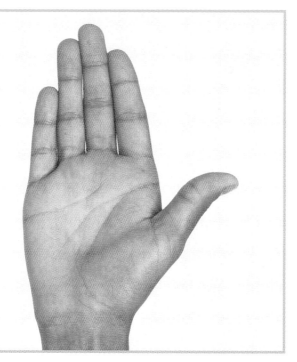

Biometric hand geometry systems look at the shape of a person's right hand. Some other systems look at a person's palmprints (similar to fingerprints).

Systems looking at the shape of the hand use information, such as finger lengths and heights, to recognize people. In fact, there are said to be over 90 different measurements that a **hand geometry system** takes. Other systems focus just on the shape of a few fingers.

As well as being one of the earliest biometrics to be measured, the hand is still one of the most successful. This is perhaps because the systems are so easy to use – a person only has to put their hand on a reflective plate, normally with their fingers between guiding pegs. These types of system are also very effective in 'dirty and noisy' areas, such as factories. Other biometrics, such as fingerprints, can be difficult to measure if the person has grease or dirt on their fingers.

Veins

The vein patterns on the back of people's hands and wrists are said to be unique. **Infrared light** is normally used to light up the hand, and then special cameras pick up the resulting images.

One of the advantages of using veins to recognize people is that it is very difficult to **forge** a vein pattern, because the veins are hidden under the skin. The vein pattern also remains the same, as it is hard to damage in everyday life.

Another advantage of vein recognition systems is that they can be made to check whether the hand is alive or not. Crime storywriters have written about the possibility of cutting off somebody's hand or finger and using the severed limb to fool the biometric system. Although this is not very realistic anyway, some systems would not be fooled, as they can tell whether a person's blood is flowing or not!

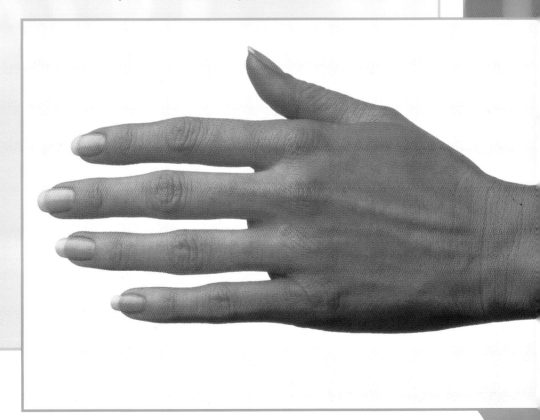

An advance in recent years has been the ability to make machines that can recognize people from the pattern of veins in the back of their hands.

Face

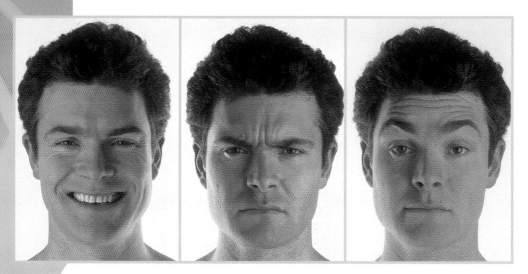

While it may be obvious to the human brain that this face is the same in all three cases, it is much more difficult for a computer to deal with a wide range of facial expressions.

The human brain is still recognized as the most powerful computer on Earth. It can do many tasks instantly, while a computer would take seconds to do them. The brain is often more accurate than a computer. This is especially true when it comes to recognizing people.

When a person tries to recognize somebody else, they normally look at that person's face. It has taken many years of development to come up with a biometric system that can do the same. Part of the problem is that the human face is so flexible. A person can have many different expressions, such as smiling, frowning or crying, all of which make it difficult for a computer to recognize the face.

In order to get around these problems, designers of face recognition systems have had to come up with many clever solutions. One is to get the computer to focus on only part of the face (normally the eyes and nose). Other systems focus just on the eyes, while some look at the lips. One system that has just been launched in the UK uses special cameras to construct a **three-dimensional image** of the face. This could make the system particularly accurate in recognizing faces.

Recognition at a distance

A face recognition system can recognize people from a distance. Unlike systems where a biometric sensor must be touched, the face recognition system works using sophisticated video cameras. It can therefore be used to monitor crowds of people, perhaps checking to see if any known criminals are present. In the future, it could be used in places like airports, so the cameras would recognize you as you walked through the terminal, and your documents could be processed immediately.

There are some drawbacks to face recognition systems, however. Most systems are unable to distinguish between identical twins. Also, it is relatively easy to avoid having your face picked up by a camera, by wearing a large hat or by looking away from the camera, for example.

Face recognition systems are extremely good at recognizing people from a distance using surveillance cameras like this one. One big advantage is that they never get tired of looking, unlike a human.

Eye

Manufacturers of biometric systems are interested in two parts of the human eye – the **iris** and the **retina**. Both of these biometrics are unique, and it has been claimed that an **impostor** has never been able to copy them successfully.

The iris and retina of both eyes are different from one another, even for identical twins. They also remain the same over a person's lifetime, only being affected by a small number of diseases. Also, the eyes are one of the first parts of the body to decay after death. This makes it highly unlikely that somebody could extract a person's eye and use it to gain access to something illegally.

Although this set of identical twins would be difficult to tell apart, their eyes would give the game away. Every person alive has a different iris and retina pattern.

The iris

The iris is the coloured ring that surrounds the **pupil** in the eye. It is made up from many different features, and is very complex. Iris recognition systems use a special camera to capture these and other features, in order to recognize a person.

When iris recognition systems were first developed, they required a person to put their eye quite close to a sensing device. Today, the technology has improved to allow recognition from at least an arm's length.

The retina

The retina is the area at the back of a person's eyeball that is sensitive to light. The blood vessels on the retina are highly complex, and unique to each person. In the 1950s, a man called Dr Paul Towers studied identical twins. He said that the pattern of veins in the retina provided more differences between twins than any other characteristic.

However, the location of the retina at the back of the eyeball makes it quite difficult to obtain an image of it. Retina scanning devices shine a low powered infrared light on the back of the eye, and then measure the pattern that is reflected. This normally requires a person to put their eye close up to a device. For some people, this process is uncomfortable and so, despite its accuracy, retinal recognition is not very widely used. However, it is expected that more user-friendly devices will be available in the near future.

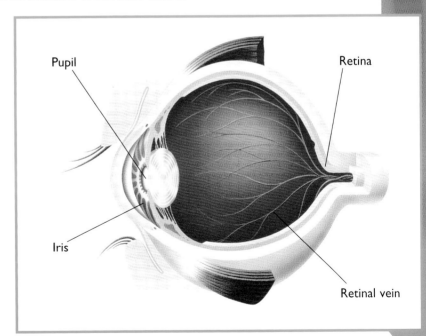

The retinal veins seen here can be viewed by shining a low power infrared light through the pupil. The retinal pattern is extremely unique and well protected throughout a person's life. This makes it an ideal biometric.

Voice

Some biometric systems use the sound of voices as a way to recognize people. Voice is a very natural biometric to use – after all, we use it to make conversation every day! We are also used to speaking into objects such as telephones, or perhaps even into a microphone. This means that people generally find systems that measure voice characteristics very acceptable.

Unlike all the biometrics discussed so far, the voice is not a distinct part of the body. It is created by the dimensions of the **vocal cords**, mouth, throat, and the cavities of the nose and teeth.

Could a voice recognition system be fooled by a professional **mimic**, or by replaying a tape recording of somebody's voice? More often than not, this would be impossible. A mimic may be able to recreate the *sound* of somebody's voice, but he or she would not be able to exactly reproduce that voice. A top quality recording of someone's voice might fool a voice system. However, you would look a little odd carrying around professional recording equipment in order to capture a person's voice! Also, many systems ask the person to say something different each time, making a standard recording useless.

The voice patterns produced by a person are created by the unique structure of that individual's vocal cords, mouth, throat, teeth and nose cavities. Here a scientist works on a recognition system.

Behavioural biometrics

Behavioural biometrics is a group of biometric systems that focuses on the way a person does something, rather than on physical characteristics. The most popular of these biometrics is a signature recognition system, but another popular method looks at the way a person types on a keyboard.

A signature recognition system does not work by looking at how a signature appears; it looks at how that signature was written. This might include the amount of pressure applied by the pen, the speed with which the signature was written and the number of times the pen is lifted from the paper. This makes it a very difficult biometric for an impostor to copy.

Signature systems have traditionally needed special pads for a person to write on, but thanks to advances in science, the technology can now work using a surprisingly normal-looking pen, without the need for any pad.

Keyboard-based biometrics look at the rhythm of a typist. They look at certain characteristics, such as the time it takes to write a password, the amount of time each individual key is pressed for and the amount of time it takes to move from one key to the next.

Checking fake signatures

Experts are able to study handwritten documents in order to check whether or not they are genuine. As well as checking for fake signatures or documents, handwriting experts often give opinions in a court of law on typed papers, the time a document was written and the age of the ink used.

A biometric signature recognition system, however, will look at different factors, such as the speed of writing and pressure of the pen. It will also do this as the signature is written, rather than sometime after the writing has been done.

A working system

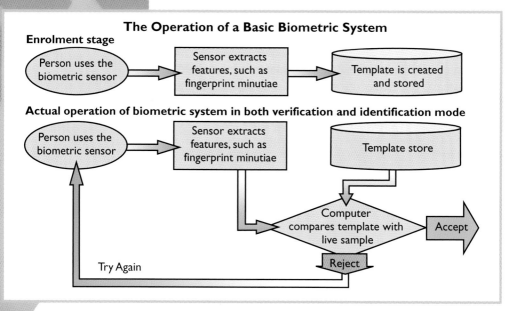

The Operation of a Basic Biometric System

Enrolment stage

Person uses the biometric sensor → Sensor extracts features, such as fingerprint minutiae → Template is created and stored

Actual operation of biometric system in both verification and identification mode

Person uses the biometric sensor → Sensor extracts features, such as fingerprint minutiae

Template store

Computer compares template with live sample → Accept

Reject

Try Again

This flow diagram shows how a basic biometric system works. There are two stages – enrolment and actual operation. The enrolment stage is necessary to create a template that can be used for future verification of a person's identity.

When a person uses a biometric system for the first time, the whole process may feel very strange and quite often they may do the wrong thing. This is quite normal, and often an experienced person will be with them to give advice on how to use the system. After a short while, most people find that the technology is so easy to use that they prefer it to whatever method they used in the past.

Using a biometric system is quite easy. All a user really has to do is present the appropriate part of their body when asked to (or in the case of a behavioural system, they must type or write a sample piece of text for the **sensor** to measure, for example). The system will then scan the biometric and extract all the relevant information, such as the shape of a person's fingers or the position of the **minutiae** on a person's **fingerprint**. This information is turned into a mathematical code by a computer. This code is called a biometric **template**, and is unique to that person. The person will not normally even notice that they are being scanned.

Enrolment

Before a person can use a biometric system, they must be **enrolled**, normally by a trained administrator. For most applications, the person must first give some form of identification, such as a passport or birth certificate, to prove who they are.

The next enrolment step is to scan the person's biometric, such as their fingerprint, to create their template. The computer stores this template for later use. Usually the system will ask the person to provide several templates, in case any are unsatisfactory. For example, a person may provide a fingerprint image that is slightly blurred, or may stutter when talking into a microphone.

The next time the person uses the system, the computer checks their new biometric sample against the template it has already stored on file during enrolment. If these match, then the person is recognized, allowing them to enter a door, access files on a computer, get money from their bank and so on. If the template and the new sample don't match, then the person is rejected. However, they are normally allowed more than one chance to be successful.

Enrolling into this biometric system involves scanning a finger for its print. The computer then analyses the image.

Where to store the template

When a person enrols into a system, an individual template is created from their biometric data. This template can be stored in a number of different places. One option is to store it in the biometric scanner itself. Alternatively, it can be transferred to a separate computer **database**. Another option is to store it on a card belonging to the person, such as a bank card or a work pass.

For some people, not all these options are appealing. Although a biometric cannot be stolen, it may be possible for someone's biometric template to be stolen by computer hackers, or misused by the owner of the system. Although there are usually safeguards against this, some people still do not like the idea of their template being stored in a separate database.

Imagine how convenient it would be if you could get out money from a cash machine without having to remember a PIN number.

Getting it wrong

Although biometric systems are extremely accurate, unfortunately none are perfect. There is always a small element of chance that a system will either falsely turn you away, or that it will let an **impostor** in, even though he or she is not registered on the system. This is where a biometric differs from things like passwords or **PIN numbers**, which are either right or wrong.

If a system lets somebody in that it shouldn't, then this is called a false acceptance. If it turns somebody away that it shouldn't, then this is called a false reject.

If a bank decided to use a biometric system to check the identity of its customers before giving them money, it would want there to be a very low number of false rejects. Otherwise, its customers would get fed up and go to a different bank, because they were always having trouble getting at their money. If you were the owner of a nuclear power station, you would want an extremely low number of false acceptances, and preferably none at all.

The table below gives examples of applications where a high number of false rejections would be unacceptable or acceptable:

Unacceptable	Acceptable
Cash machine manufacturer	Military installation
Mobile phone manufacturer	Nuclear power station
Car manufacturer	Airport security
Leisure park operator	Bank safe

The people on the left hand side of this table would find a high false reject rate unacceptable because their customers would soon get fed up with the technology getting it wrong. For the locations on the right hand side of the table, it is absolutely essential that the biometric technology does not let somebody in by accident. In order to get this level of security, people will understand if the system is very sensitive and rejects them a few times (as long as it recognizes them eventually!).

Identification or verification

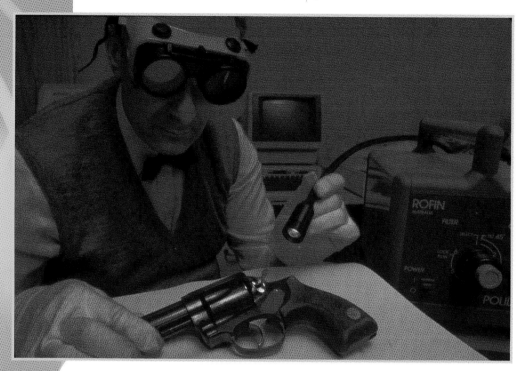

The police can search a crime scene, or objects involved in a crime, for any fingerprints that may have been left behind by the criminal. These prints can then be checked against police files to see if a match exists.

Sometimes, biometric systems are used to identify a face in a crowd of people, or a person's fingerprints that have been picked up at the scene of a crime. When a biometric system doesn't have any information as to who that person is, it must check the biometric template against all the others in its files, which is much harder to do. This process is called **identification**. Systems that use this process tend to be more expensive, because they need a large amount of computer power to search through all the records – sometimes there are hundreds of thousands.

This is distinctly different from the way most biometric systems work. Normally, the biometric system only has to check a person's biometric against one template stored on file – it is only checking that you are who you say you are. So if a person gives their name to the system, it checks if the record stored under that name is the same as the one you are now presenting. If they are the same, it accepts you. This process is called **verification**.

AFIS systems

The most common type of identification system uses fingerprints. These are called **Automatic Fingerprint Identification Systems (AFIS)**. They are used by police forces around the world to try to catch criminals from fingerprints left at crime scenes.

In some countries, AFIS systems are also being used to check that people can't claim social **benefits** using a false name. If a person goes to the benefit office saying they are not already claiming benefits, their fingerprints can be checked against all the other fingerprints in the computer. If the AFIS system finds a match, then there is a very high chance that the person is already claiming benefits, and is trying to cheat the system.

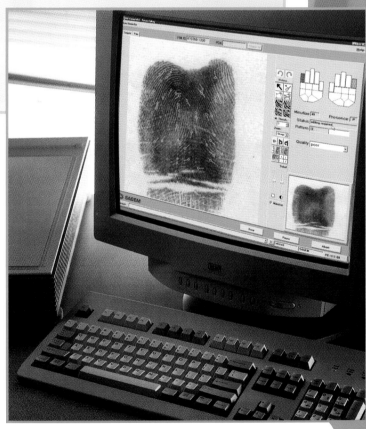

AFIS systems speed up the fingerprint checking procedure greatly. What sometimes used to take days can now be done in a matter of minutes or hours.

Biometrics in real life

New uses for biometric technology are being found all the time. Over the last few years, it has been used for everything from checking the identity of people calling a home shopping television channel, to making sure that athletes at the last two Olympic Games in Atlanta and Sydney were secure in their accommodation.

If you think about it, anywhere that requires a key or anything that needs a password could be secured by a biometric system. This means that cash machines, mobile phones, doors, computers, jails, hospitals and even entire countries can be protected by biometric systems.

As the biometric industry grows, how its technology can be used may become more obvious. One of the first places you might notice the technology is on computers. Many new computers already come with microphones and web cameras, and these will increasingly be used to perform face and voice recognition in the future.

Banking

Many banks around the world are watching the development of biometrics. Some have even installed a biometric system. Cash machines with **iris** recognition cameras have been tested in the UK. In the USA, **online banking** services, using a computer mouse with a **fingerprint** scanner, have been issued to a large number of customers as a trial.

Telecommunications

Mobile phones are easy to steal, and so have become a main area of interest for biometric companies. Putting something like a fingerprint **sensor** on a mobile phone would make it useless to a thief. Alternatively, voice recognition systems have been used to identify customers checking their bank balances over the telephone. Customers of the UK's Nationwide Building Society recently tried out this type of system, and found it easy to use.

Immigration

It could be possible to make entire countries secure with biometrics. Some people are already looking at adding biometric information to passports. In the USA, many international airports allow people who travel by aeroplane regularly to use hand recognition systems, so that they can avoid long queues at passport control. In the UK, all **refugees** have their fingerprints checked to see if they have asked to live in the country before. This means that the authorities can immediately identify refugees who are not genuine.

Olympic success for biometrics

At the Olympic Games in Sydney, Australia, in 2000, security was a very strong concern for the organizers.

Biometrics were chosen to provide high security for the German Haus area of the Olympic Complex. A system that used iris recognition technology was installed. It would only let people in if they were successfully identified. In total around 1200 people, including the athletes, media and other officials, were able to use the system.

Before anybody could use the system, they first had to be **enrolled**. This took place in Germany before the Games started. Once at the Olympics, the enrolled athletes simply had to focus an eye on to the reader in order for it to be recognized. They were then allowed access to the complex.

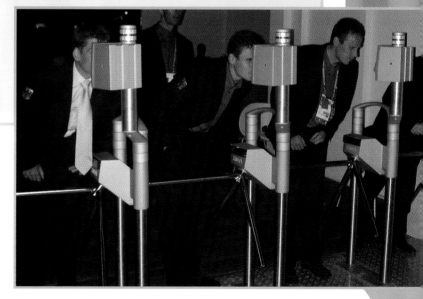

Athletes at the last two Olympic Games had the opportunity to use iris recognition technology as they accessed their accommodation.

Welfare

Unfortunately, **fraud** is a problem in most countries that give money to their citizens when they become unemployed, ill, have children or become pensioners. Sometimes people try to apply illegally for **benefits** by pretending to be somebody else or by claiming in more than one town. Biometric technology can detect these people by comparing their biometric against a central **database**. In areas where this system has been set up, fraud has fallen dramatically.

One of the first recorded uses of biometrics for welfare began in South Africa in 1989, when pensioners started getting their pensions using biometrics to prove their identity. The scheme was specifically designed for pensioners living in remote areas, who couldn't easily get to a town to collect their money. Instead, several hundred vehicles were sent out to these pensioners, equipped with two cash machines and fingerprint sensors. Because of the country's rugged terrain, many insects and extremes of temperature, this equipment does not have an easy life!

Physical access control

Biometric systems were first used to prevent people entering restricted areas. Today, biometrics are being used to protect the security of everything from schools to banks. The problem with **PIN numbers**, keys and **swipe cards** is that they can be stolen, or easily lost. Biometrics are attractive because they solve all these problems.

Computer security

The use of computers in the world is growing at an astonishing rate. This has lead to a society where many **transactions** have moved from the real world to the 'virtual' world of the Internet. Today, business contracts are signed over e-mail, company shares are traded online and even music and books can be bought online. The problem with the Internet is that it is not very secure – that is, it is sometimes possible for people to gain access to personal information about you over the Internet, without your knowledge or permission. Biometric systems are being proposed which could help improve computer security, not just for Internet transactions, but also for stopping people accessing your computer without permission.

Healthcare

There are few things that are more private than a person's health records. Imagine the outcry if these ended up in the wrong person's hands. Biometric companies are coming up with ways to help prevent this, particularly when these records are stored on a computer.

Medical records hold extremely secret information about you, so it is vitally important that this information is kept secure. Today, many doctors are looking at biometric technology to make records even safer.

Law and order

The police are extremely interested in biometric technology. It can help them identify criminals by their fingerprints and it can help to make certain areas, like prisons, secure. However, law and order also includes checking the identity of voters and the giving of **national ID** cards to people. Many countries give their citizens ID cards. Sometimes, however, these cards are seen as a threat to people's freedom.

A large national ID scheme using biometrics has started being used in the Philippines. Cards will eventually be given to around 63 million citizens, each with the individual's fingerprint data stored on the card. The card will be used for voting, for proof that a person lives in that country and for general **identification**.

Safer streets?

Facial recognition technology is being used in certain areas of London, in an attempt to spot known criminals walking the streets. The system, which uses closed circuit television (CCTV) cameras, has been in place since 1998. It has supposedly led to a reduction in crime of around 40 per cent.

The CCTV cameras capture images of people's faces, which are sent back to a main control room and fed into a central computer. This computer holds photos of certain types of known criminals. In order to be on the local database, the criminals must be living in the local area, there must be police intelligence that they have committed a crime in the past twelve weeks and they must have been prosecuted at some point in the past for a criminal act. The computer compares the captured face image against the computer records, and if it matches, an alarm sounds. An operator in the control room then checks to see if there is really a match and only then will police officers be alerted.

Some people see this type of system as a threat to people's privacy. However, signs in the area alert the residents to the use of the technology there. Also, the system immediately deletes the faces it has

captured if they do not match anyone on file, so the police do not have the ability to check up on anybody but known criminals. Parents can also ask for the system to look out for missing children. The local population has wholeheartedly accepted the system in this part of London, where something like 0.04 per cent of people cause 90 per cent of the crime.

If criminals know they are being watched by powerful face recognition technology they are much less likely to commit a crime in that area.

Walt Disney

In the USA, Walt Disney is using biometrics to confirm the identity of season ticket holders at a variety of its theme parks. The Disney system is well received by visitors, who are aware that biometric technology is being used to identify them.

The Magic Kingdom, Epcot and Disney MGM all make use of a **finger geometry system**, instead of issuing a photo passport to their visitors. Once the index and middle fingers of a visitor's hand have been measured, that visitor's **template** is stored in a computer system which links to all the parks.

Visitors are issued with a paper ticket that contains information about them on the back. When a visitor next goes to one of the parks, he or she presents their ticket. This is then used to call up their original template from the central computer. The visitor presents his or her fingers to the device, and it compares them with the computer template. A Disney spokesperson said that visitors were at first surprised with the system, but once they discovered how easy it was to use (and what fun!) they were delighted.

Some theme parks are taking advantage of biometrics to admit season pass holders. This does not just cut down on waiting times for the visitor, but is fun, too.

Coming soon

The newer biometric systems that are coming on to the market are not just designed for high security uses or for governments and powerful companies. Today, the price of the technology has come down far enough to allow it to be used in everyday items such as mobile phones, computers and cars.

Imagine a world where you are able to walk up to your car and **automatically** open the door just by gripping its handle. Then once you are inside, you are able to start the engine with the tip of your finger. In fact, the computer inside the car will recognize you as a registered owner of the car, and will also remember all of your favourite settings and adjust them automatically, such as the ideal position of your seat, mirrors and your favourite radio station. This technology is almost possible today, and is one of the uses of biometrics that will almost certainly hit the market in the next few years.

It is likely that more cars will soon use biometric technology to recognize their owners, like this one here. This would put an end to the need for car keys.

To most people, biometrics seems a very futuristic technology. They are often surprised, therefore, to find that they could be using the technology in their everyday life very soon! It is certainly reasonable to assume that biometric technology will become even more widespread within the next five years.

Studies have shown that consumers find biometric technology exciting, and **manufacturers** of products such as cars and telephones are always looking for technologies that will make their products more appealing.

Mobile phone security

Mobile phone manufacturers are interested in the added security that biometrics could bring to their products. There is a real problem of mobile telephones being stolen, so anything to prevent this would be welcome – if somebody did steal a biometrically secured mobile phone, it would be useless to them.

Many different types of biometric could be used with a mobile phone. Instead of having to remember and type a security **PIN number** into the phone, a user could just present their biometric. Some of the biometrics being considered include **fingerprints**, face, **iris** or voice.

Phone manufacturers wanting to use face or iris recognition would have to have a small camera built into their phone first.

Mobile phones using biometrics could become widespread over the next few years. Not only would they be more secure, they'd also look very stylish!

Biometrics in use

Places such as offices, supermarkets, airports and even casinos could be revolutionized by new biometric technology. Not only that, but there are products coming on to the market that could actually help save lives in the future, such as the smart gun.

Elsewhere, even some children's toys use biometrics. In the USA, for example, products have been launched ranging from a lockable diary that only opens when it recognizes its owner's voice, to bedroom alarms that sound if anybody but the recognized owner tries to enter. In fact, there are not many areas of life that biometric product manufacturers have left out in their plans to make biometrics more widespread.

In the Netherlands, nightclubs are using face and fingerprint recognition technology to monitor 'clubbers' coming through their doors. This helps them spot previous troublemakers on their files, who they can then choose to turn away. Police, meanwhile, are able to monitor crowds at football matches to try to cut down on potential violence.

Airports

One area that has received a lot of interest in recent years is the use of biometrics in airports. Some airports in the USA, for example, have been using biometrics to help cut down queues at passport control. People that are **enrolled** into a special airport biometric system can bypass the long queues by proving their identity using their bodies rather than a passport. The most common biometric for passengers to use is their hand shape.

More recently, however, the focus has been switched toward using biometrics to help identify suspect individuals. The shocking **terrorist** attacks, which used planes as missiles to strike at targets in the USA on 11 September 2001, will probably lead to the further use of biometrics in airports.

In particular, facial recognition technology will be used alongside airport surveillance cameras. Facial recognition is good because it can identify known suspects from crowds of people at a distance. However, the technology is not foolproof and will only be a part of the overall airport security systems. It would possibly be more accurate if used in a certain area, such as passport control, where all passengers must pass before boarding a plane.

The smart gun

Each year, a large number of people are killed through the accidental firing of guns. Sometimes, police officers can lose their guns in a struggle and their guns can end up being used by criminals. In the USA, police officers are already beginning to use 'smart guns', which will only fire if they are being held by an authorized user. The smart gun below will only fire if it is being held by a user in possession of a special microchip.

Meanwhile, biometrics companies are racing to produce the world's first **commercial** biometric smart gun, which would use a small biometric **sensor** in the gun's handle to identify the user. In the wrong hands it would be entirely useless. Gun companies are said to be very interested in the prospect of such a gun.

A smart gun will only fire if it is being held by a registered user.

Advantages and disadvantages

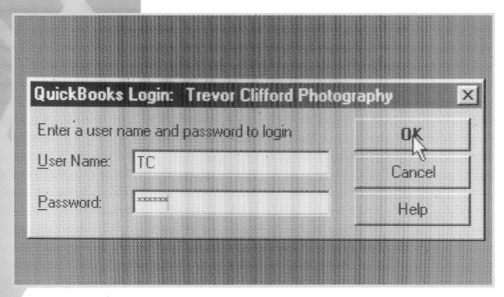

Biometric technology could replace passwords on computers.
Some people have to remember numerous passwords as part of
their jobs. This is not always easy to do without writing them
down, which of course makes them easy to steal.

One of the greatest advantages of biometric technology
is that it can link a person to his or her actions. Once a
biometric system is put in place, it becomes impossible
for a person to deny that they accessed the company
computer, or opened the door to the safe. Other
technologies, such as passwords or keys, can be stolen,
borrowed, copied or even guessed.

The first biometric systems were seen as a way to
increase security. However, there are other benefits for
people using biometrics. These days, for example, people
have to remember many more passwords, especially on
computers. Everything from e-mail accounts to school
exam results tend to be protected with passwords. People
may be able to remember three or four passwords, but
beyond that, they have to start writing them down – often
on pieces of paper, which they then unwittingly stick on
to their computer monitor or desk! A biometric could
be used instead of all these passwords, eliminating this
problem. Similarly, it would mean that people would never
have to carry around large bunches of keys, or memorize
PIN numbers for using cash machines at banks.

Buddy punching

Biometrics are not only secure and convenient – they can also help companies save money. If you imagine a large company with thousands of workers, it is an almost impossible task for managers to check whether their workers are turning up on time and staying for a full **shift**.

A lot of companies try to solve this problem by having '**clocking in**' and '**clocking out**' systems, where a worker stamps a time card at a machine as they turn up to work each day. However, there is nothing to stop a worker's colleague from illegally stamping their card for them. This problem is called 'buddy punching', and can cost companies a great deal of money.

An increasing number of companies are adding biometrics to their existing **attendance systems**. This means that a worker has to be present when they clock in and out. Effectively, using biometrics makes 'buddy punching' impossible, saving the company money.

A worker 'clocking in' at work. Biometrics could help prevent 'buddy punching', where a colleague illegally stamps a friend's time card so that they will be paid even though they have not turned up for work.

Disadvantages

Most technologies have numerous advantages, but also have possible drawbacks. Take the mobile phone as an example. While it may be extremely useful, because you can speak to people wherever and whenever you like, a drawback is that people can listen to your private conversations. Also, they don't always work properly because of poor reception.

Biometric technology has similar disadvantages. Some people feel that by using biometrics, their privacy could be invaded. Also, it is a well-known fact that biometric systems do not always work perfectly. As we have seen in earlier chapters, it is quite possible that a system will reject a user even though it is not supposed to.

The cost of biometric systems is another possible drawback of the technology. However, prices have come down dramatically in recent years. This trend is also likely to continue, thanks to increasing **economies of scale** as more and more systems are made.

In most societies people are entitled to privacy. Some people, however, worry that their private biometric information could be used improperly by those who hold it, if it is used more widely, for example to secure mobile phones.

An invasion of privacy?

Some people warn that biometric technologies could pose a threat to a person's right to privacy. They fear that a person's biometric data could be accessed, and somehow used against them.

While such a situation would of course be an invasion of privacy, it is most unlikely to actually happen. For a start, biometric **templates** are normally **encrypted** to stop anybody from being able to view them. Also, even if these templates could be viewed, they would be of little use, because they do not actually show the original **fingerprint** or **iris** image.

In most cases, biometric technology is helping to increase privacy by preventing the wrong people from seeing personal information, such as bank account details or **medical records**.

> 'It is hard to imagine what extra mischief the state could get up to with this [biometric template] information, compared to the volumes of information they already hold on you – except of course to accurately assign you to such already held information.'
>
> Julian Ashbourn, author of *Biometrics: Advanced Identity Verification – The Complete Guide*, 2000

Codes and encryption

Since ancient times, people have tried various ways of making information into codes. A code could be very simple – for example, substituting letters in a message with different letters, according to certain rules. If the rule says letters in the alphabet must be shifted one place to the right, then A becomes B, B becomes C and so on. So, the word BIOMETRICS would become CJPNFUSJDT. If another person knows the rule, then they can easily read the original message; if not, then it could take a very long time to work it out!

Modern day coding is known as encryption. It uses complex rules to create almost unbreakable codes. All sorts of information are encrypted today, such as credit card details on the Internet. Biometric template information is often encrypted, making it virtually useless to anyone if they managed to steal it.

Access denied!

It is possible that a person will not be able to **enrol** into a biometric system. For example, if that person is blind, they may find it impossible to register on an **iris** recognition or **retina** system. Alternatively, a person could have lost a limb, or in rare cases they may not even have a **fingerprint**.

To a certain extent, biometric technology suppliers have thought about these issues. Perhaps people who could not enrol in a biometric system would be allowed to use a password to access their computer, or use a **smart card** to access a building. Sometimes a biometric system can register a different biometric to the one it is supposed to register.

Clearly not every biometric technology is suitable for every person to use. A blind person, for example, would have great difficulty using an eye-based technology. Biometric system designers must always bear these limitations in mind.

Most people should have no problems enrolling, especially if they are given professional help when they first use the system. People with biometrics that are particularly difficult to measure may need extra attention at the enrolment stage. Otherwise, they could find it difficult to use the system later on.

False rejects

Assuming you have enrolled into the system and are looking forward to using it for the first time, what happens if the system doesn't recognize you? Does this mean you will never be allowed to access your bank account again, or that nobody will believe that you are really you?

Of course, the answer is no. Normally, the biometric system will give people numerous attempts to be accepted. Often people may press too hard on a **sensor**, or they may speak too early or quickly into a microphone. Bearing this in mind, a little care and patience should ensure that a biometric system will not reject people.

In any case, people would still be able to prove who they really are through the many documents that they have today – their passport, birth certificate or identity card, for example – although this would obviously be an inconvenience.

Multiple biometrics

Some biometric systems use more than one biometric to identify a person. These are called multiple biometric systems. With this type of system a person might have to present both their fingerprint and voice pattern, or their face and their hand. Sometimes a system might even register three biometrics together.

This type of biometric system can sometimes be advantageous. For example, if a person cannot easily use one type of biometric device, such as a fingerprint reader, then the system could still use the other biometrics to identify that person. A drawback might be that the system is trickier to use.

Opting out

The question of opting out of biometrics altogether sometimes comes up. What if, for various reasons, you do not want to use biometric technology? Will you be allowed to opt out, or will you be forced to use the system?

The answer is both yes and no. It is important to understand that there are biometric systems where you can opt out of using the technology, and others where the technology has to be compulsory.

All **commercial** applications of the technology are optional. For example, nobody would force you to buy a mobile phone with a biometric sensor on it. Likewise, if your bank started using biometrics and you didn't approve, you could always change banks!

Claiming benefits is one area where compulsory use of biometrics would be necessary. Experience shows that the introduction of a biometric system dramatically reduces **fraud**. This is partially because the fraudsters are caught out, but also because as soon as people know they could be caught they stop trying to claim benefits illegally.

Compulsory biometrics

However, there are times when a biometric system has to be used by everybody, or it would not work effectively. Imagine a person who regularly posed as someone else to claim additional **benefits** from the government. If this person were given the option to enrol into a biometric system, then obviously he or she would choose not to. This would defeat the object of using biometrics at all, as the small number of cheats would not choose to enrol, and so would never be caught.

Clearly, when biometric technology is used on certain groups of people (prisoners, for example) they will not have the option of opting out. However, in other places, such as offices, the company management will usually be legally obliged to get their employees to agree to using the technology before installing a system.

In the commercial world, biometrics are marketed as being highly beneficial to the consumer. Although people are able to choose not to use biometrics, they most likely will be tempted because of all the added security and convenience the technology will bring.

The table below shows examples of applications where biometrics, if used, would be compulsory or voluntary:

Compulsory	Voluntary
Prison	Mobile phones
Government social benefits	ATM machines
Asylum seekers	Cars
Military bases	E-commerce

Controversial technology

The biometrics industry faces significant opposition from certain groups of people. Some believe that biometric systems are an invasion of personal privacy, as these systems must store a person's unique characteristics on file. Other groups of people believe that biometric systems go against certain religious beliefs.

There are even people that, for hygiene reasons, do not want to place their hands or fingers on a device that has been touched by others – even though it is no more dangerous that gripping a door handle.

The biometrics industry has to contend with all these concerned groups of people and make sure its systems do not cause undue alarm. Of course, this industry is not alone in having its critics. The motor industry, for example, has many opposition or **pressure groups**, wanting new technology to make cars safer and so on.

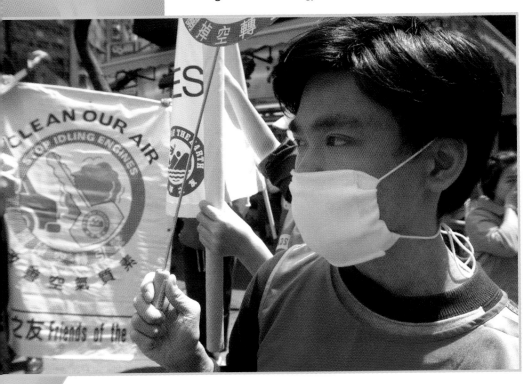

Pressure groups can sometimes be helpful in persuading industries to introduce safer or more responsible technology.

The presence of these groups can often help to shape the industry in a more acceptable way – hence the motor industry's development of air bags to ensure the safety of car passengers. In the same way, the biometrics industry is introducing safeguards to ensure that the technology is used responsibly.

'As soon as biometrics leaves the laboratory and we enter the real world, then these concerns must be faced and answered.'

Yona Flink, Opticom Technologies in Israel

Orwellian technology

George Orwell's famous book *Nineteen Eighty-Four* tells the story of a time when the government had complete control over the population, and knew at all times what people were doing. Today's politicians are very aware that they would be accused of being **'Orwellian'** if they were to do anything that seemed too dominating or controlling.

Some people would see the introduction of a nationwide biometric system as Orwellian. This is one concern that governments have to consider, despite the advantages such a system could bring in terms of reducing **fraud**. Explaining how biometric technology works, as well as explaining its advantages and limitations, is a necessary step if a biometric system is to be successfully introduced.

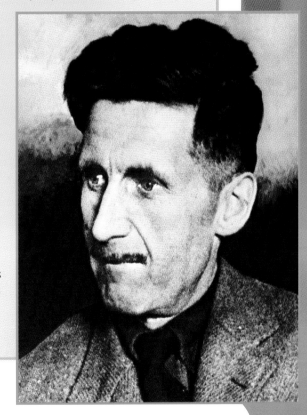

George Orwell dreamt up a world where the government was 'all powerful'. Today, any technology that gives governments power to monitor its citizens is sometimes referred to as 'Orwellian'.

Religious concerns

Religion is not a major issue when it comes to the use of biometrics, but there are certain groups that fear biometric technology because it could relate to verses written in The Bible's Book of Revelations.

'He forced everyone small and great, rich and poor, free and slave, to receive a mark on his right hand or on his forehead.'

Book of Revelations, chapter 13, verse 16

The Bible contains references to 'the mark of the Beast' and how this will either be placed on a person's right hand or forehead. There is a small proportion of people who are concerned that this refers to the use of biometric technology, and so the **manufacturers** of one hand recognition device tried to address this issue. The company advised:

'Our scanners do not in any way have the ability to detect the "mark of the Beast" or any other mark on a person's hand and do not in any way have the ability to place the "mark of the Beast" or any other mark on a person's hand… We suggest that any individual having concerns regarding the "mark of the Beast" be **enrolled** and use the hand scanner with their left hand turned palm up.'

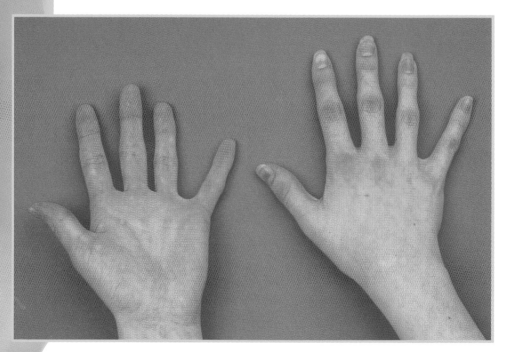

An upturned left hand would work in a **hand geometry system**, even though the machine is normally designed to operate using the right hand turned downwards.

The company advised concerned people to use their left hand turned upwards. This is because its scanners will only usually work with the right hand, due to the position of special guiding pegs on the machine. These fixed pegs, which are designed to fit at the bottom of the V-shape existing between a person's fingers, would not be in the right position if the left hand was used. However, by turning the left hand upwards, the pegs would be in the right position again.

There are other potential conflicts between biometrics and religion, although these are not to do with a fear of biometric systems. For example, some of the Arab population have headwear that can cover a portion of the face, while many women who follow the religion of Islam must cover almost all of their faces. Clearly, for these people, the use of facial recognition systems would be inappropriate.

Although religion does not play a large role in biometrics, some religions make it difficult to use certain biometric technology. For example, facial or eye-based recognition would not work when a person's face is obscured.

Into the future

Although the biometrics industry's origins can be traced all the way back to ancient times, the modern industry is still in its early stages. It is really only in the last 20 to 30 years that progress has been made to bring the technology out of the laboratory. Today, biometric systems have developed far enough for them to be used in everyday life.

There are many biometric technologies that are now established, such as **fingerprint**, **iris** and voice recognition. In the future, others will probably be developed that will also be successful. These might include automatic **DNA** analysis, earprint recognition and recognizing people by the way that they walk. This last biometric could be particularly useful in helping to recognize people who wear a mask whilst holding up banks or shops. Other biometrics and cameras would be no use in this situation.

This thief had better be careful. Although face recognition systems wouldn't recognize him because he is wearing a mask, some systems will be able to recognize a person by the way they walk!

No doubt even more bizarre technologies will be dreamt up in the future. Some people have suggested that technology able to recognize people from their unique chemical odours could be developed – although quite what people would think of a machine sniffing them is uncertain! It wasn't too long ago that iris recognition was seen as a futuristic technology, yet today its use is becoming more and more widespread. Most of the newcomers will not be realistic, but who knows, some may develop to become the technology of tomorrow.

Earprints?

The earprint may not seem like an obvious biometric to use to recognize people, but it is actually already being used to capture criminals in some areas. In countries where there are a large number of high-rise apartment blocks, like Switzerland, thieves find it difficult to know if anybody is at home or not. In order to find out, they often put their ear up to the front door to listen for signs of movement. This can leave an earprint, which may be used to identify the criminal in the same way as a fingerprint.

Although this practice is far from widespread, it could become more common in years to come, if large **databases** of criminals' earprints were built up.

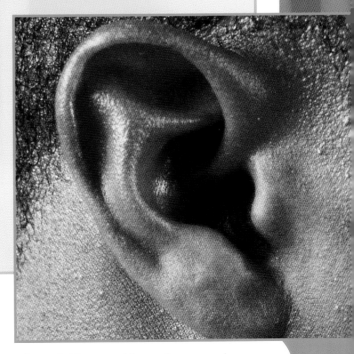

Remarkably, some biometric systems have great success in identifying people from earprints left behind at the scene of a crime.

Futuristic applications

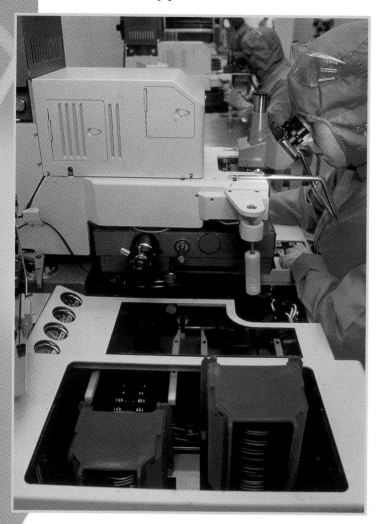

The development of microchip technology means that biometric systems will become even cheaper. This could lead to widespread use of the technology in the future.

The number of possible uses for biometric technology is almost endless. Biometrics are already being used everywhere from schools to hospitals, and this range will continue to expand. Where the technology will be used in the future, however, is difficult to predict.

Much depends on the price, and consumer opinions of the technology will be crucial. If consumers decide that they like biometric technology, then it will very quickly be used in goods such as cars, telephones and personal computers.

Good news for parents

Biometrics could eventually be used with television sets. With the rapid growth of satellite and cable television and its home shopping channels, it will soon become possible to buy everything from food to films without ever having to leave your seat.

While this may be very convenient, it could also be easily abused. For instance, a child may suddenly decide that he or she wants to buy all the latest toys without permission, or a teenager may not be able to resist the latest pair of expensive trainers! Using biometrics would ensure that only the person paying for the goods would be able to access the system and shop.

Home and away

As the price of biometric technology comes down further, it is even possible that the technology could replace the traditional keys and locks in people's homes. This would be a valuable boost for the biometrics industry.

Away from the home, biometric technology is starting to be used in places such as football stadiums (to ensure hooligans don't get in) and even high street shops to allow customers to pay for goods, or to alert staff to the arrival of a loyal customer as they walk into the shop.

The future certainly holds great promise. Over the next few years, biometric technology will become more widespread, and it is possible that people will say they couldn't even remember life without biometrics!

Timeline

2600BC Egyptians use body measurements to identify workers building the Great Pyramids.

1800BC Babylonian kings are said to use hand imprints
–600BC to prove the authenticity of certain engravings and works.

1684 Nehemiah Grew at the Royal Society in London, UK, notices that people's **fingerprints** can be classified into different pattern types.

1823 Jan Evangelista Purkyně, a Czech, realizes that no two fingerprints are the same.

1879 Alphonse Bertillon joins the Paris Police Force in France, and quickly develops an advanced measurement system for prison inmates.

1880 Henry Faulds, a Scottish doctor living in Japan, publishes his thoughts on the variety and uniqueness of fingerprints, suggesting that they could be used for the **identification** of criminals.

1882 The first recorded use of fingerprints for identification in New Mexico, USA.

1892 Alphonse Bertillon becomes the first director of the Paris Bureau of Identification in France. He quickly develops a system for classifying people using all sorts of human body measurement.

1894 Mark Twain, the famous author, publishes a book called *Pudd'nhead Wilson*, in which fingerprint identification is used to catch the murderer.

1896 A national fingerprint system is established by Juan Vucetich, an Argentinean police officer.

1900 The Galton-Henry system of classifying fingerprints is published.

1901 A Fingerprint Branch at the UK's Scotland Yard, lead by Sir Edward Henry, is established.

1903 The famous case of the Will Wests, who are found to have identical body measurements, but different fingerprint patterns. This leads to the end of the Bertillon measurement system.

1930s Research is published suggesting that blood vessels in the **retina** could be used to identify people.

1950s Dr Paul Towers investigates identical twins and says that the retinal vein pattern provides the biggest difference between them.

1960s	The first true biometric system is released. Developed by the Miller Brothers in New Jersey, USA, the system is a mechanical device that **automatically** measures the length of people's fingers.
1970	Pioneers at the UK's National Physical Laboratory first develop a reliable statistical method for signature **verification**.
1970s	The company Identimation launches an electronic version of the mechanical hand reader called the IdentiMat. Texas Instruments is a pioneer in speech verification. Its development program dated back to the 1960s, and the company is awarded a series of contracts by the US Air Force to produce voice-based security systems.
1975	Five fingerprint readers are developed and installed at the FBI in the USA by Rockwell International.
1978	First **AFIS (Automatic Fingerprint Identification System)** systems are installed for the Royal Canadian Mounted Police and the Florida Police Department in the USA.
1985	The first retinal scanning units are launched by a company called EyeDentify.
1987	One of the first signature verification systems, developed by Rod Beaston, is sold.
1989	One of the first welfare systems using biometrics is established. It is used when handing out pension money from mobile cash points, to confirm the identity of those pensioners living in remote areas of South Africa.
1993	The first trial of the now widespread INSPASS immigration scheme takes place at Newark International Airport in New Jersey, USA. This uses **hand geometry** to confirm the identity of frequent passengers flying into the USA.
1995	Iridian Technologies launches the first system to identify people from their **iris** patterns.
1996	Three Walt Disney Parks in Florida, USA, use **finger geometry** to **verify** visitors holding a seasonal pass.
1998	The UK launches a face recognition system in parts of London to check for known criminals. A 40 per cent reduction in crime is claimed.
1999	The Home Shopping Network in the USA launches a speaker verification system to confirm the identity of its customers on the telephone. The system is claimed to be the largest ever use of biometrics.
2000	The Sydney Olympics in Australia uses biometrics to secure certain areas of the athletes' village.
2001	Police at the US Super Bowl use facial recognition technology to check for known criminals in Tampa, Florida, USA. The system recognized nineteen people.

Glossary

arch common fingerprint pattern, which can either look like a mound or be pointed like a steeple in appearance

attendance system system that checks to see when employees turn up to and leave work

automated something that operates without direct human control

Automatic Fingerprint Identification System (AFIS) system that compares a fingerprint against the whole database of stored prints and gives a list of the most likely matches. They are normally used by law enforcement agencies.

automatically performing an action without human intervention

behavioural biometric a biometric arising from the way a person does something

behavioural characteristic unique trait of a person that can be measured, such as the way he or she signs their name or types at a keyboard

benefits financial aid given by the government to various groups of citizens, such as pensioners or the unemployed

Caucasian person with light-coloured skin

clocking in/clocking out a system used by employers to note the time workers arrive and leave work. Often there is a machine that stamps the time on the worker's time card.

commercial available to buy

database store of information in a form that can be handled by a computer

DNA thin, unique molecule in the form of a twisted ladder, found in every living cell on Earth. Also known as deoxyribonucleic acid.

economies of scale economic term that says that cost savings occur by making a product in greater quantities

encrypt to put information into a code so that only the person (or computer) with the right key can decode it

enrolled when a person's biometric characteristic is measured and registered into the biometric system

finger geometry system system that recognizes a person from the shape of their finger, similar to a hand geometry system

fingerprint the complex network of lines on a person's finger

forensic using science to help with legal investigations

forge to make an imitation or copy

fraud criminal deception

hand geometry system system that recognizes people from the shape of their hand

identification process of checking a biometric template against all the others in a database. More generally, identification means establishing a person's name, age, nationality, often with a document.

impostor person who pretends to be somebody else

infrared light light that is not visible to the human eye as it has a wavelength slightly longer than visible light rays at the red end of the light spectrum

iris coloured ring at the front of the eye that surrounds the pupil

loop fingerprint pattern where the fingerprint ridges start at one side of the finger, loop around at the tip of the finger, and come back to the same side they started on

manufacturer company that produces goods with machinery

medical record stored, historical information regarding a person's health

mimic person that is good at reproducing the actions of another person, including the sound of their voice

minutiae tiny irregularities in the fingerprint pattern, which are useful for identification

national ID document or card that is given to a country's citizens for proof of identity

online banking the process of accessing your bank account details and making transactions via a computer connected to the Internet

Orwellian word stemming from George Orwell's famous book, *Nineteen Eighty-Four*, meaning an overpowering government

paper essay written for the academic community

physical biometric unique part of somebody's body that can be used to recognize them

PIN number personal identification number that is normally four digits in length. They are often used at bank cash machines.

pressure group organized group of people that tries to influence government policy through action and publicity

provisions supply of food and drink

pupil opening in the centre of the eye, which allows light to pass through to the retina

refugee person who has fled their home country to live elsewhere

retina membrane layer at the back of the eyeball that is sensitive to light

sensor the device (a microphone, for example) that actually measures a person's biometric

shift specific period of time that a set of workers will work

smart card card, like a bank card, containing a small microchip for storing and processing information

swab specimen of fluid taken from the body using an absorbent pad

swipe card plastic card, like bank a card, with a black magnetic strip on the back, which is read by swiping it through a machine

template unique mathematical code created from the image of a person's biometric

terrorist person who uses violence or intimidation, especially for political purposes

three-dimensional image an image with length, width and height

transactions actions that are performed, often relating to business, such as purchasing an item for money

verification process of checking a person's template against one other stored in the database

verify to check the truth of something, in this case that a person is who they say they are

vocal cords the main sound producers in human beings. They consist of two small folds of tissue, which stretch across the voice box.

whorl pattern on the fingerprint which is normally circular or spiral in shape

Sources of information

Organizations

The Association for Biometrics, www.afb.org.uk

The Association for Biometrics represents the biometric community, organizes many meetings and publishes information on a variety of biometric subjects.

The Biometric Consortium, www.biometrics.org

The US government created the Biometric Consortium in 1994. The government uses it as a focal point for research, development, testing, evaluation and application of biometric technology.

Forensic Press, www.forensicpress.com

A free resource for students, parents and school resource officers, with lots of fun and free information on fingerprints.

The International Biometric Group
1 Battery Park Plaza, New York, NY 10004, USA,
www.biometricgroup.com

The International Biometric Group is a company of consultants that focuses on the biometric industry. Its website contains a lot of information on how biometrics work.

The International Biometric Industry Association
601 Thirteenth Street, NW, Suite 370 South, Washington DC
20005, USA www.ibia.org

The International Biometric Industry Association was founded in 1998 and is a high profile lobbying group for the biometric industry. Its website offers a lot of good advice on the biometrics industry and the issues it faces.

Privacy International, www.privacyinternational.org

Privacy International is a human rights group formed in 1990 as a watchdog on surveillance by governments and corporations. The group is based in London, and also has an office in Washington, D.C. It conducts campaigns throughout the world on a range of privacy issues.

Further reading

Books on biometrics are published mainly for professionals interested in the subject. The following books and documents are quite advanced but give information on the history of the subject, the way the different technologies operate, how the technology is used in real life and the size of the market for biometric technology.

Biometrics: Advanced Identity Verification – The Complete Guide, Julian Ashbourn (Springer-Verlag, 2000)

The Biometric Industry Report: Market and Technology Forecasts to 2003, Mark Lockie and Farzin Deravi (Elsevier Science, 2001)

Biometrics and Law Enforcement, a document by Clive Reedman. Obtain a copy by emailing Creedman@btinternet.com

Index

Titles in the *Science at the Edge* series:

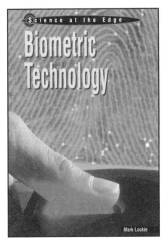

Hardback   0 431 14885 6

Hardback   0 431 14882 1

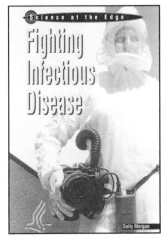

Hardback   0 431 14884 8

Hardback   0 431 14883 X

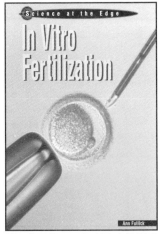

Hardback   0 431 14881 3

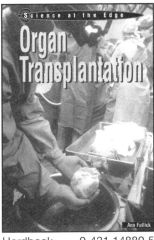

Hardback   0 431 14880 5

Find out about other Heinemann Library titles on our website www.heinemann.co.uk/library